THE RIGHT TO VOTE

AMERICAN INDIANS' RIGHT TO VOTE

by Liz Sonneborn

pogo

Ideas for Parents and Teachers

Pogo Books let children practice reading informational text while introducing them to nonfiction features such as headings, labels, sidebars, maps, and diagrams, as well as a table of contents, glossary, and index.

Carefully leveled text with a strong photo match offers early fluent readers the support they need to succeed.

Before Reading

- "Walk" through the book and point out the various nonfiction features. Ask the student what purpose each feature serves.
- Look at the glossary together. Read and discuss the words.

Read the Book

- Have the child read the book independently.
- Invite him or her to list questions that arise from reading.

After Reading

- Discuss the child's questions. Talk about how he or she might find answers to those questions.
- Prompt the child to think more. Ask: What did you know about American Indians and their right to vote before reading this book? What more would you like to learn about this topic?

Pogo Books are published by Jump!
5357 Penn Avenue South
Minneapolis, MN 55419
www.jumplibrary.com

Library of Congress Cataloging-in-Publication Data

Names: Sonneborn, Liz, author.
Title: American Indians' right to vote / by Liz Sonneborn.
Description: Minneapolis, MN: Jump!, Inc., [2025].
Series: The right to vote | Includes index.
Audience: Ages 7-10
Identifiers: LCCN 2024002127 (print)
LCCN 2024002128 (ebook)
ISBN 9798892131490 (hardcover)
ISBN 9798892131506 (paperback)
ISBN 9798892131513 (ebook)
Subjects: LCSH: Indians of North America–Suffrage–Juvenile literature. | Voting–United States–Juvenile literature. | Indians of North America–Government relations–Juvenile literature. | Citizenship–United States–Juvenile literature.
Classification: LCC E93 .S659 2025 (print)
LCC E93 (ebook)
DDC 324.6/208997–dc23/eng/20240215
LC record available at https://lccn.loc.gov/2024002127
LC ebook record available at https://lccn.loc.gov/2024002128

Editor: Alyssa Sorenson
Designer: Molly Ballanger
Content Consultant: Dr. Walter C. Fleming (Kickapoo Tribe in Kansas), Professor of Native American Studies, Montana State University

Photo Credits: RichVintage/iStock, cover (man); Mega Pixel/Shutterstock, cover (sticker); YinYang/iStock, cover (sign); RichLegg/iStock, 1; ImagePixel/Shutterstock, 3; LPETTET/iStock, 4; SDI Productions/iStock, 5 (people), 6-7; Kameraworld/Dreamstime, 5 (ballot); MelWood/Shutterstock, 8; Christine_Kohler/iStock, 9; 3LH-Fine Art/SuperStock, 10-11; Bettmann/Getty, 12-13, 16-17; piemags/NSC/Alamy, 14-15 (foreground); donatas1205/Shutterstock, 14-15 (background); Elaine Thompson/AP Images, 18; Danita Delimont/Alamy, 19; US Interior Department/Alamy, 20-21; Reid Dalland/Shutterstock, 23.

Printed in the United States of America at Corporate Graphics in North Mankato, Minnesota.

TABLE OF CONTENTS

CHAPTER 1

TO THE POLLS

U.S. **citizens** pick their leaders. How? They vote. They do this during **elections**.

People fill out **ballots**. They pick **candidates** they like. The votes are counted. The people with the most votes win. They become government leaders.

polling place

Many people vote at **polling places.** Others mail their ballots. People can vote after they turn 18 years old.

Voting is important. Why? U.S. leaders make big decisions. People want leaders who support the same things they do.

Some people have not always been able to vote. For many years, American Indians were not U.S. citizens. They could not vote. They did not have a say in how the country was run.

CHAPTER 2

GETTING THE VOTE

American Indians have lived in North America for thousands of years. Each **nation** has its own unique **culture**.

Navajo dancer

In the 1500s, Europeans came to North America. Some got along with American Indians. Others fought them for land.

The United States formed in 1776. The government took land from American Indians. It made them leave. Many American Indians had to live on **reservations**. Some U.S. leaders did not want them to be citizens. Why? American Indians had different ways of life. Leaders did not like that. They wanted to stop them from voting.

TAKE A LOOK

How much land did the U.S. government take from American Indians? Take a look.

1776

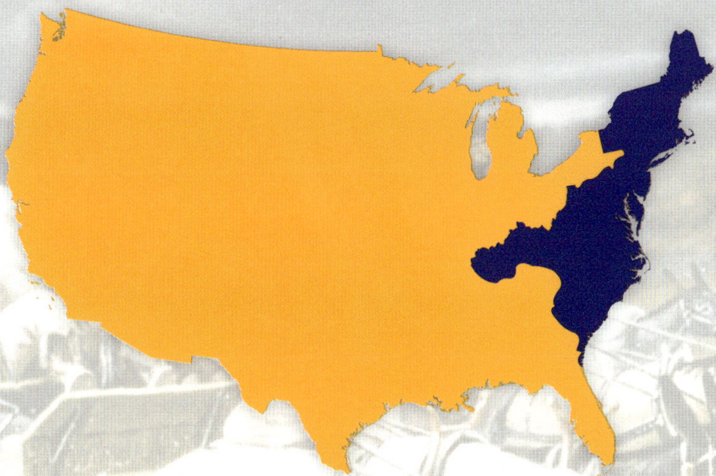

2024

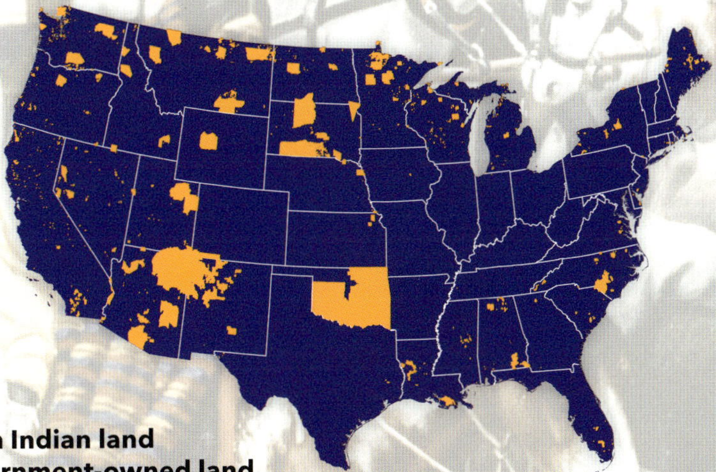

American Indian land
U.S. government-owned land

Zitkala-Sa

The government treated American Indians badly. People spoke up. Zitkala-Sa was part of the Yankton Sioux Tribe. She wrote about her life. In 1918, she spoke to people. She talked about the right to vote. Voting could change things. She wanted to be a U.S. citizen. She also wanted to celebrate her culture.

WHAT DO YOU THINK?

Some American Indians did not want the right to vote. They did not want to be U.S. citizens. Why do you think they felt this way?

Some American Indian men were soldiers in World War I (1914–1918). They helped the United States. They wanted to vote. In 1919, the U.S. government let them. Then in 1924, it passed a law. The law made all American Indians citizens.

Bridgehead
Grenze
Kopf Coblenz
AMERICAN
AMERIKANISCHE

Some states did not want them to vote. They tried to stop them. They made rules. Like what? American Indians had to pay to vote. Some had to pass unfair tests. White people also **threatened** them. They made many American Indians afraid to vote.

The government passed the Voting Rights Act in 1965. It ended these practices. Finally, American Indians could vote in U.S. elections.

WHAT DO YOU THINK?

Is it important to let everyone vote? Why or why not?

CHAPTER 3

ISSUES TODAY

Voting can still be hard. Some American Indians live far from polling places. They travel hours to vote. Some mail their ballots. How? They put them in drop boxes. But many have to drive far to mail them.

Some state laws make voting hard. People may need a **voter ID** to vote. The ID must have a street address. Why? It proves where a person lives. But many people on reservations do not have street addresses. They cannot vote.

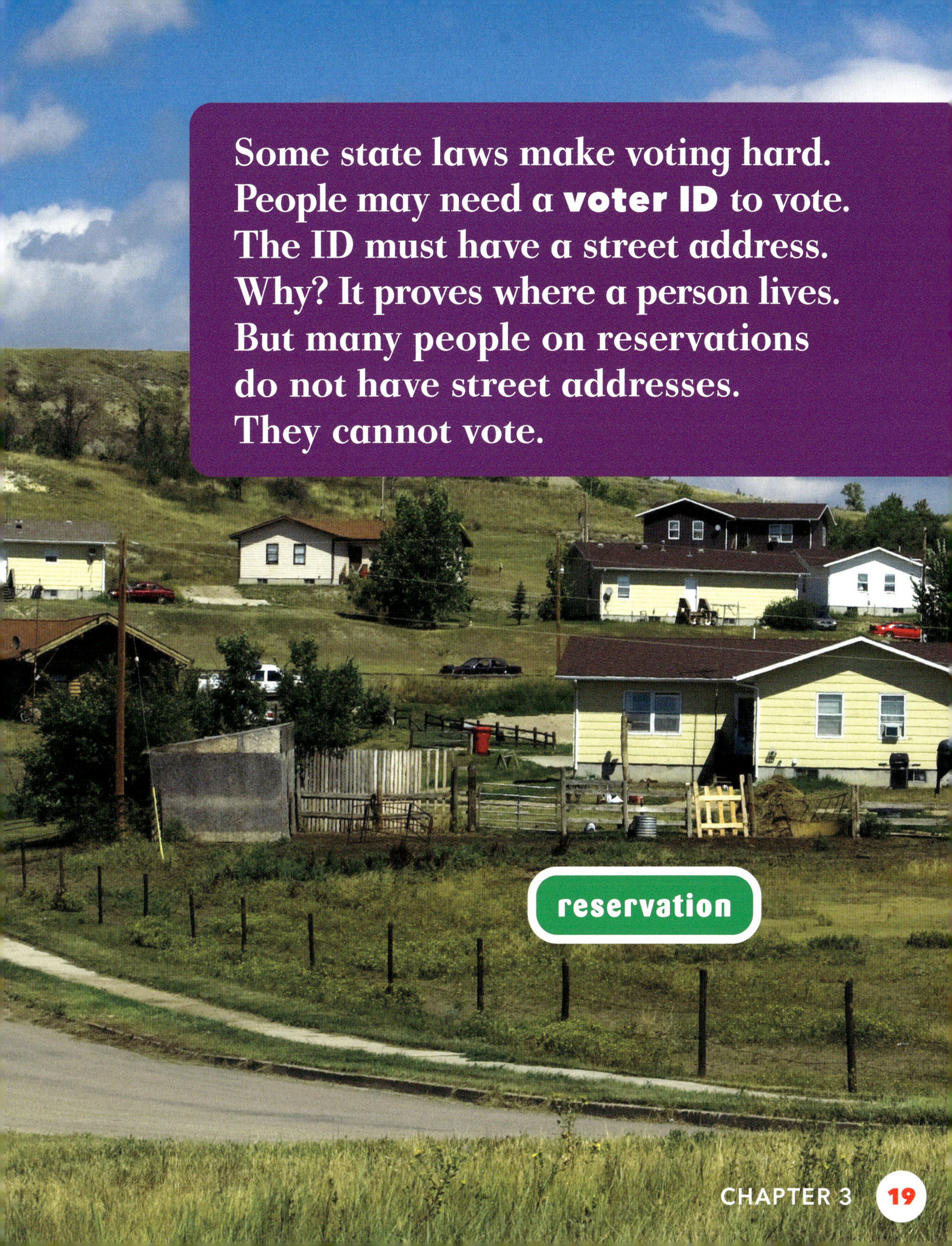

People work for change. They take part in **lawsuits**. They work with U.S. leaders. They support **bills**. These bills would make voting easier for American Indians. They work to make their voices heard.

DID YOU KNOW?

The U.S. government recognizes 574 American Indian nations. Each has its own rich history and **traditions**.

TE HOUSE
TIONS SUMMIT

QUICK FACTS & TOOLS

TIMELINE

American Indians have faced many struggles and successes when voting in the United States. Take a look.

1776
The United States forms. The government doesn't let American Indians become citizens.

1887
The U.S. government passes the Dawes Act. Some American Indians can now be citizens, but they have to give up their traditional ways of life.

1919
American Indians who served in World War I get to vote.

1924
The Indian Citizenship Act passes. It makes all American Indians U.S. citizens. States still make it hard for them to vote.

1965
The Voting Rights Act stops many state laws that keep American Indians from voting.

2021
The Native American Voting Rights Act bill is introduced. If turned into a law, it will make it easier for American Indians to vote.

GLOSSARY

ballots: Pieces of paper that people use to mark which political candidates they want to hold office.

bills: Written plans for new laws that are debated and passed by legislators.

candidates: People who run for office in an election.

citizens: People who belong to a country and have full rights.

culture: The ideas, customs, traditions, and ways of life of a group of people.

elections: The acts or processes of deciding something by voting.

lawsuits: Legal actions or cases brought against a person or a group in a court of law.

nation: A group of people that shares a culture, language, or ancestry.

polling places: Buildings or locations at which people vote.

reservations: Areas of land American Indians kept and that some live on today.

threatened: Said they would hurt or cause trouble for someone.

traditions: Customs, ideas, or beliefs that are handed down.

voter ID: A type of identification that can be used to verify who someone is.

INDEX

TO LEARN MORE

Finding more information is as easy as 1, 2, 3.

1. Go to www.factsurfer.com
2. Enter "AmericanIndians'righttovote" into the search box.
3. Choose your book to see a list of websites.

FACT SURFER